SCIENCE WIDE OPEN
Women in Botany

Written by Mary Wissinger
Illustrated by Danielle Pioli

Science, Naturally!
An imprint of Platypus Media, LLC
Washington, D.C.

What's inside a seed?

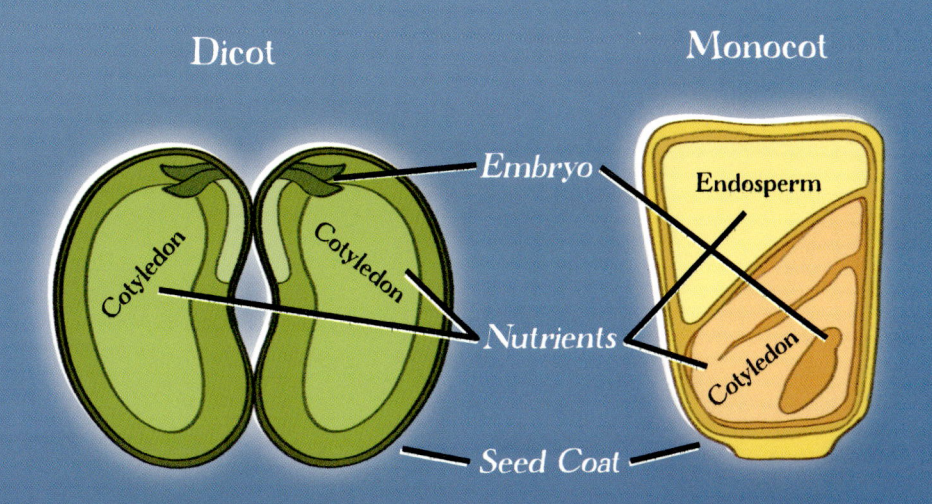

Dicot

Monocot

Embryo

Endosperm

Cotyledon

Cotyledon

Nutrients

Cotyledon

Seed Coat

Inside a seed is a plant waiting to happen. From the smallest of flowers to the tallest of trees, most plants on the planet come from seeds.

A seed coat keeps the seed cozy and safe. A baby plant, called an embryo, is snuggled inside along with nutrients for the plant to sprout.

Waheenee paid attention to seeds. She had the important job of growing all the food for her family and helping to feed her community.

She knew exactly when to plant sunflower seeds in the spring. She sprouted squash seeds in a mixture of grass and leaves before sowing them in the field. In the autumn, she saved enough corn seeds for two seasons of planting, just in case a harvest was bad.

Waheenee / Buffalo Bird Woman
(*wah-HEE-nee*)
Mandan, Hidatsa, & Arikara Nation, ca. 1839–1932

As Waheenee tended her crops, the seeds grew into the plants that fed many people. Waheenee used traditional ways of planting that had been passed down for generations, even after she and her people were forced to leave their homeland. She shared her people's history and planting methods in books that were written about her life. Just like her, we rely on seeds to grow into the fruits, vegetables, and grains we eat every day.

How does a seed become a plant?

Every seed needs a few things to become a plant:
water, light, the right temperature, and space
to grow. When the seed is ready, it sends roots
down into the soil. Then a stem grows up toward
the light. You can see the plant when the stem
pops through the soil.

There are some plants that have always grown well in gardens and on farms. But others grow best in the wild. When Elizabeth Coleman White was a girl, blueberries only grew wild in the forest. They were often hard to find.

Elizabeth dreamt of a whole field of blueberries that she could easily pick. It seemed impossible. Many people had already tried and failed to grow blueberries on farms.

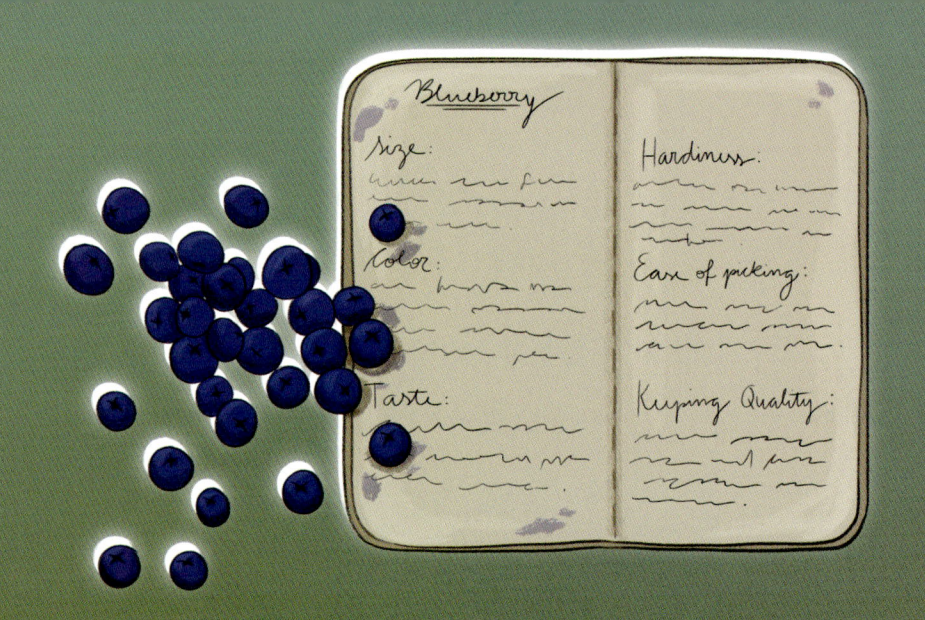

Elizabeth used botany—the scientific study of plants—to make her dream come true. She planted blueberry bushes in soil that she and her research partner had specially prepared.

After lots of hard work, she figured out how to grow blueberries on her farm! She sold them at markets, sent cuttings of bushes all over, and became known as the Blueberry Queen. Thanks to Elizabeth's persistence, blueberries are now grown and eaten all around the world.

Elizabeth Coleman
(ee-LIZ-ah-beth KOHL-man)
United States, 1871–1954

We eat plants, but what
do plants eat?

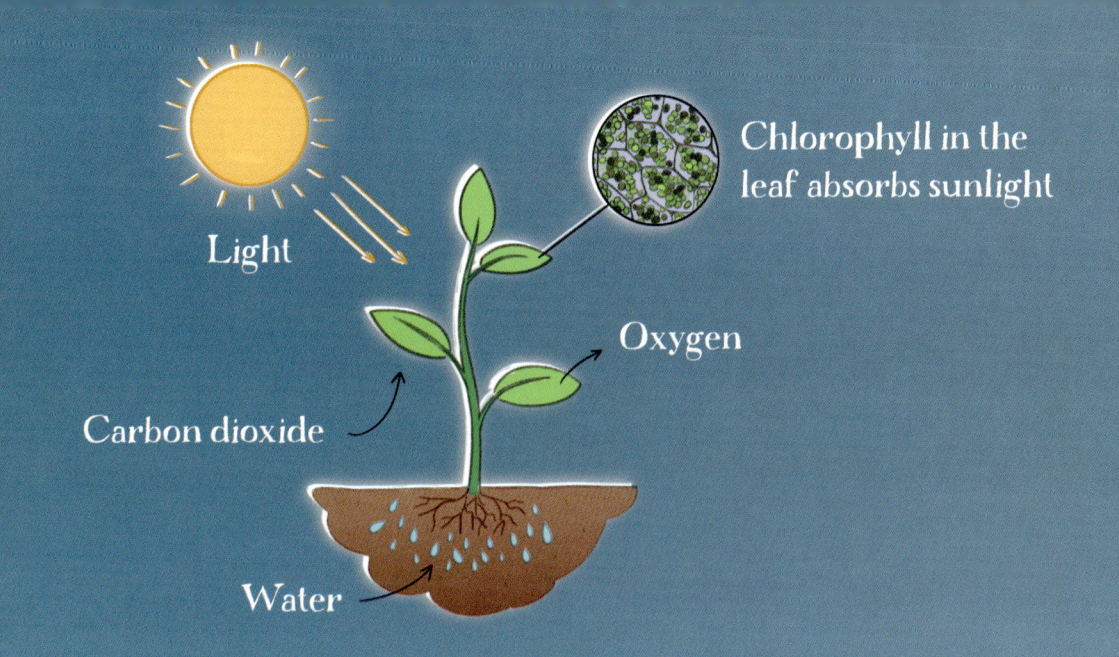

Light

Chlorophyll in the leaf absorbs sunlight

Oxygen

Carbon dioxide

Water

Plants make their own food through a process called photosynthesis.

Plant leaves have a pigment, or coloring, that makes them green. It's called chlorophyll, and it absorbs light energy from the sun. That energy is used by the plant to help it combine water and carbon dioxide, which produces food. Photosynthesis also makes oxygen, which the plant releases through its leaves. That oxygen becomes an important part of the air we breathe.

The incredible process of photosynthesis is one of the many reasons botanists travel the world studying plant life.

Ynés Mexia was 51 years old when she began her global search for plants. Whether she had to cross a bog, canoe down a river, or camp out for months, she was determined to collect plants. Her passion made her unstoppable: she continued her expeditions even after she fell off a cliff!

Ynés Mexía
(ee-NEHZ meh-HEE-ah)
United States, 1870–1938

Mexianthus mexicanus
Collected Dec. 1, 1926

Ynés had an excellent memory that helped her quickly spot new plants. She collected almost 150,000 plant specimens to study. Some people dream of discovering just one new species of plant. Ynés discovered as many as 500 new species, many of which are named after her. Her work gave us a better understanding of plants and added to the Linnaean System.

What's the Linnaean System?

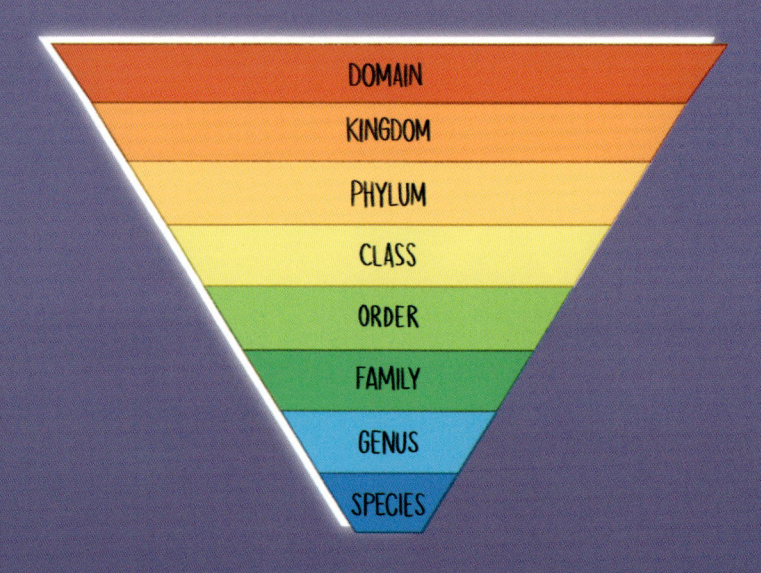

Just like a library organizes books, the Linnaean System organizes all life forms on Earth. It gives a scientific name to every plant that has been discovered. It also acts like a family tree, showing us how plants are related to one another.

Almost 400,000 different species of plants have been found on Earth so far, and they can be full of surprises.

Eelgrass and other
marine plants live in saltwater.
Tiny wildflowers dot the icy tundra.
Mosses are found in almost every
ecosystem on Earth and can even grow
in sidewalk cracks. Giant sequoia trees
live thousands of years and grow as tall as
31-story buildings. No matter where or
how plants grow, the Linnaean System
keeps track of them all. As we
organize and study the plants
that support life on Earth,
we learn more ways
they help us.

How do plants help us?

Plants give us so many things: food, water, dye, protection from the elements, healthy soil, shade, and even medicine.

Long ago, Loredana Marcello's palace gardens were filled with beautiful plants. She ran experiments with the plants and used them as herbal medicines. When people in her city got very sick during the plague pandemic, Loredana's medicines helped them feel better.

In Loredana's time, herbal medicines were some of the only medicines available. Sometimes plants were boiled in water for a sick person to drink. Plants could also be dried and crushed, then mixed with fats to make ointments. Some traditional remedies are still used today, such as ginger for an upset stomach, or aloe vera for a sunburn.

Loredana Marcello
(*LOR-eh-DAHN-ah mar-CHELL-oh*)
Venice, Italy, ca. 1533–1572

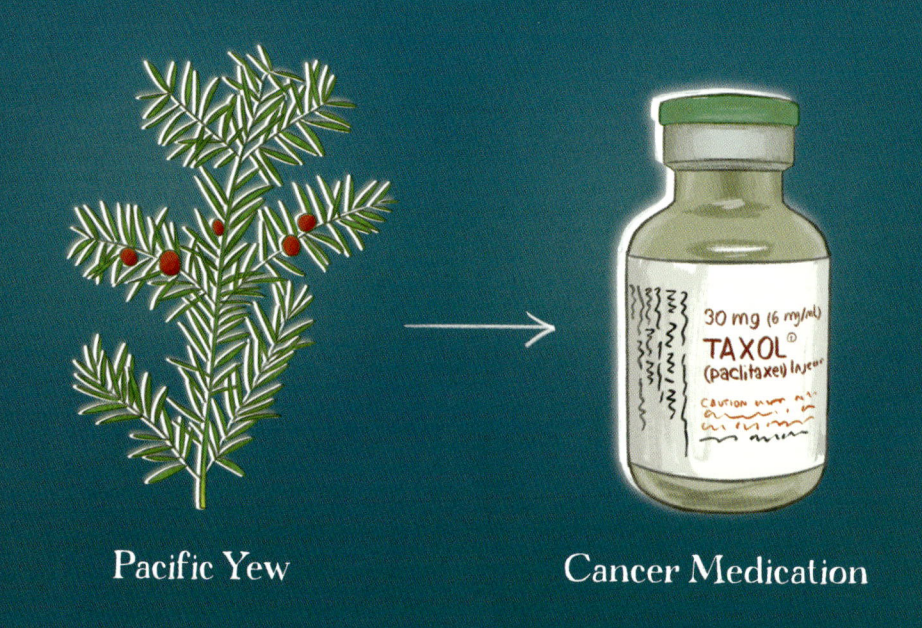

Pacific Yew

Cancer Medication

Modern medicines look different than the herbal ones Loredana made, but many of them still come from plants. Plants are used to create medicines that lower fevers, reduce coughs, relieve pain, heal wounds, fight infection, and even treat cancer. Botanists today are still finding ways to use plants, and even make new plants.

How do botanists make new plants?

Pollen

Stamen

Petals

Petals

Pistil

Dr. Janaki Ammal spent years creating new plants called hybrids. These combinations of different plant varieties can be difficult to make, but she enjoyed working in the laboratory. She even had a squirrel that kept her company.

Dr. Janaki faced a big challenge: creating a new sugarcane hybrid that would grow well in India. She tried many times before a hybrid was successful. The new, sweeter, hybrid sugarcane she created is still enjoyed across the country today.

Dr. Janaki Ammal
(JAH-nah-KEE ah-MALL)
India, 1897–1984

INDIA

Later, Dr. Janaki led the Botanical Survey of India. The project worked to document and study every type of plant in the country. It was a big job: India is over a million square miles (that's almost three million square kilometers). She scoured the country for plants. She also fought to protect plants and preserve natural areas from development.

LEAVE NO TRACE
NATIVE PLANT
HABITAT

Why is it important to protect plants?

Plants are important for the health of Earth's environment. They provide a home for animals, fungi, insects, and many of the living things that support our planet's delicate ecosystems. When one part of the environment suffers, other parts suffer too.

Dr. Wangari Maathai saw what happened when too many trees were cut down in the rainforest. The soil dried up and people couldn't grow enough food. Animals lost their shelters and sources of food. Stream water evaporated in the hot sun.

Dr. Wangari started the Green Belt Movement to change things. She taught women in Kenya how to grow trees from seeds, and the women were paid to plant trees all around the country.

As the trees grew, the soil healed, and food could be grown again. Animals returned to safety, and tree shade let streams flow once more. Dr. Wangari also led classes to strengthen and protect the small communities that relied on the trees.

Not everyone wanted Dr. Wangari to speak out for the environment or fight for human rights. She was even arrested, but she kept planting trees. Dr. Wangari's world-changing work earned her a special award called a Nobel Peace Prize. Today, the Green Belt Movement she began has planted over 50 million trees and improved the lives of many people.

Dr. Wangari Maathai
(wahn-GAH-ree mah-THAIY)
Kenya, 1940–2011

Plants give us so much!

Yes. Plants are powerful. They make life on Earth possible. They nourish our communities, improve our health, shelter and feed animals, heal and protect the environment, and make the world more beautiful.

Give plants space to grow, and incredible things can happen. All it takes is a handful of seeds.

Glossary

BOTANY: The scientific study of plants, including where they are found and how they interact with their environment, as well as their growth, structure, classification, and uses.

CARBON DIOXIDE: A gas produced by humans and other living things when we breathe out. It is used by plants during photosynthesis to create food.

CHLOROPHYLL: The pigment that makes plants' leaves green. It absorbs light energy from the sun.

COTYLEDON: A part of a seed that stores nutrients for the embryo and becomes the first leaves for the plant. Cotyledons are sometimes called "seed leaves."

CUTTINGS: Partial sections of a plant from which a new plant can grow.

DICOT: A type of seed, like a bean, that has two cotyledons.

ECOSYSTEM: The community of living organisms in a habitat that all interact with and depend on each other.

EMBRYO: The part of a seed that develops into a plant.

ENDOSPERM: A part of a seed that stores nutrients for the embryo. In a dicot, the endosperm is absorbed by the cotyledons; in a monocot, it is separate.

HARVEST: To gather fruits or vegetables when they are ready to be used or eaten.

HYBRID PLANT: A combination of two or more varieties, species, or genera of plants.

LINNAEAN SYSTEM: A way to organize all living things into groups based on traits that they have in common.

MONOCOT: A type of seed, like a corn kernel, that has one cotyledon.

NUTRIENTS: What all living things need to eat or absorb in order to grow and survive.

OXYGEN: A gas that humans and other living things need to survive. It is released into the air by plants during photosynthesis.

PANDEMIC: The rapid spread of a disease that infects and endangers a large group of people.

PHOTOSYNTHESIS: The process by which plants make their own food from carbon dioxide, water, and sunlight.

PIGMENT: A natural material that creates color.

PISTIL: The part of a flower that forms seeds. It also catches pollen to use in the process of making seeds.

POLLEN: A powder created by flowering plants that is used to make new seeds.

RAINFOREST: A dense, tropical ecosystem with tall trees and a lot of rainfall. Home to some of the rarest plants and animals in the world.

ROOTS: The part of the plant that reaches underground to collect water and nutrients.

SEED COAT: The outer covering of a seed that protects the plant embryo.

SOW: To plant or scatter for growing.

SPROUT: To begin to grow by producing buds or shoots.

STAMEN: The part of a flower that produces pollen.

Science Wide Open: Women in Botany
Copyright © 2022 Genius Games, LLC
Original series concept by John J. Coveyou

Written by Mary Wissinger
Illustrated by Danielle Pioli

Published by Science, Naturally!
English hardback first edition • September 2022 • ISBN: 978-1-938492-58-7
English paperback first edition • September 2022 • ISBN: 978-1-938492-59-4
English eBook first edition • September 2022 • ISBN: 978-1-938492-60-0

Spanish edition coming March 2023.

Enjoy all the titles in the series:
    Women in Biology • Las mujeres en la biología
    Women in Chemistry • Las mujeres en la química
    Women in Physics • Las mujeres en la física
    Women in Engineering • Las mujeres en la ingeniería
    Women in Medicine • Las mujeres en la medicina
    Women in Botany • Las mujeres en la botánica

Teacher's Guide available at the Educational Resources page of ScienceNaturally.com.

Published in the United States by:
    Science, Naturally!
        An imprint of Platypus Media, LLC
    750 First Street NE, Suite 700 • Washington, D.C. 20002
    202-465-4798 • Fax: 202-558-2132
    Info@ScienceNaturally.com • ScienceNaturally.com

Distributed to the trade by:
    National Book Network (North America)
        301-459-3366 • Toll-free: 800-462-6420
        CustomerCare@NBNbooks.com • NBNbooks.com
    NBN international (worldwide)
        NBNi.Cservs@IngramContent.com • Distribution.NBNi.co.uk

Library of Congress Control Number: 2022937698

10 9 8 7 6 5 4 3 2 1

Printed in the United States of America.